A RAINY DAY

David Bauer
Illustrated by Jeff Hopkins

Rigby®

A Harcourt Achieve Imprint

www.Rigby.com
1-800-531-5015

We see the rain.

3

We see the books.

5

We see the hats.

We see the blocks.

9

We see the dog!

We see the mess!

We see the sun!

We see the rainbow!